SLOW COOKING

$9.99

joanna white

TAYLOR TRADE PUBLISHING

Slow Cooking, a nitty gritty® Cookbook

©2013 by Taylor Trade Publishing
An imprint of
The Rowman & Littlefield Publishing Group, Inc.
4501 Forbes Boulevard, Suite 200
Lanham, MD 20706
www.rowman.com

Produced by CulinartMedia, Inc.
Design: Harrah Lord
Layout: Patty Holden
Editor: Daniella Malfitano
Photography: Eising Food Photography (all rights reserved)
www.culinartmedia.com

Distributed by National Book Network
1-800-462-6420

ISBN 978-1-58979-881-6
Library of Congress Cataloguing-in-Publication Data on file

Printed in China

CONTENTS

THE BASICS

TIPS AND TRICKS

Slow cookers are ideal for today's busy lifestyles. Prepare the recipe the night before or in the morning, put the cooker on before you leave and have your meal ready to eat when you get home after a long day. Count the advantages and you'll go back to that slow cooker in your cupboard, or invest in a new one.

THE ADVANTAGES OF SLOW COOKING

• A slow cooker allows the cook to prepare the meal in advance.

• More nutrients are retained because of the lower temperatures used.

• One-pot meals require less cleanup.

• Food is generally juicier because slow cooking seals in moisture.

• Considerably less energy is used (less than a 100-watt bulb) when cooking on low.

• Less space is needed to cook food. Slow cooking is ideal for boats, R.V.s, cabins, and small kitchens.

• When using the low setting, you can leave without worry about having to tend the food. Low heat will not dry out or burn the food. Generally, you do not even have to stir.

• Slow cookers are ideal even in the summer because they do not heat up the kitchen.

• Exact timing is not crucial, so if you are delayed at work, your food will not be overdone.

• Slow cookers are ideal for buffets and informal entertaining because they allow you to serve directly from the pot. Use as you would a chafing dish to keep food warm or to serve hot drinks.

DO'S AND DON'TS OF SLOW COOKING

• Do not take the lid off during the cooking process unless the recipe calls for it. This will let out steam, which is used to cook the food at the top of the pot and it will take at least 15 minutes to regain that steam pressure. Also, positively never remove lid during the first 2 hours of baking in the slow cooker.

- Always allow more time when cooking at higher altitudes.

- Always bake on high.

- Low temperature refers to 200°F. High temperature refers to 300°F. If your particular brand of slow cooker has additional settings, be sure to determine where these temperature settings are so you can properly follow the recipes in this book.

- Defrost food before using in recipes. Frozen food may cause the slow cooker to crack if using a porcelain, enamel or crockery-lined pot. Also, frozen food will increase cooking time considerably.

- Be cautious when baking, where another pan is placed in the pot and water is added. Check the pot to make sure the water does not evaporate.

- Do not immerse any electrical control units or parts in water at any time.

- To maintain the finish on the inside of the pot, soak with warm, soapy water and scrub with a nylon or plastic pad.

- For easier cleanup afterwards, spray inside the pot with nonstick vegetable spray before cooking.

- Root vegetables like carrots, turnips, parsnips, rutabagas, etc., quite often take longer to cook than the meat, so it is best to layer these on the bottom and let the liquid keep the vegetables moist (which helps them cook more evenly).

- Beans are ideal for slow cookers. It is best to soak the beans overnight; discard the soaking water and then add the beans to the recipe and slow cook until beans are tender.

- Pasta and rice have a tendency to fall apart or become gummy, so add these ingredients precooked (using conventional cooking methods) at the end of the cooking time or simply serve with the dish.

- Dairy products like milk and sour cream should be added toward the last hour of cooking because slow cooking has a tendency to curdle these products.

- For best results in your slow cooker, fill pot at least half full of ingredients.

CONVERTING RECIPES TO SLOW COOKERS

- There may be variations in cooking temperatures depending on the brand of slow cooker, so first determine the proper LOW (200°F) and HIGH (300°F) temperature settings. NEVER allow the cooking temperature to drop to less than 180°F, in order to prevent spoilage or improperly cooked food.

• Generally quadruple the regular cooking in a slow cooker on low. For example, for a stew that requires 2 to 2½ hours standard cooking time, you would increase the time to 8 to 10 hours on low.

• If choosing to cook on high, double the conventional cooking time but do not leave the slow cooker unattended. You may also need to stir occasionally. 1 hour on HIGH is equivalent to 2 hours on LOW.

• Some brands have very high settings to be used for the purpose of browning meats. After browning, be sure to reduce the temperature to LOW.

• For meats that need browning, such as chicken, slow cook the food first, and then remove and brown in a hot oven or broiler just before serving.

• If you are afraid of not being able to return in time or if cooking time is less than your working day, consider investing in an automatic timer. Your slow cooker plugs into the timer that will turn on automatically after you leave. It is best not have it turn off automatically, because hot food should not be left out more than 2 hours.

• When adapting a recipe to slow cooking, you may need to increase spices. Because the food tends to lose less liquid from evaporation, the extra juiciness may require additional flavoring.

• Baking requires placing the ingredients in a separate container (like a coffee can, a pudding mold, a tall baking dish, etc.), covering with foil, tying down the foil and surrounding with water.

• For thickening sauces: Turn cooker on high; stir in thickener which has been mixed with cold water and cook 20 to 30 minutes, stirring occasionally until thickened.

Cornstarch: Use 2 tablespoons dissolved in 2 tablespoons cold water for every 2 cups of sauce that needs to be thickened.

Flour: Use 4 tablespoons dissolved in 4 tablespoons cold water for every 2 cups of sauce that needs to be thickened.

Tapioca: This is usually stirred in before cooking, so it doesn't need to be mixed with water. Use 3 to 4 tablespoons for every 2 cups of liquid used in the recipe.

Potato: Sometimes sauces can be thickened by simply adding instant potato flakes or adding puréed potatoes.

TECHNIQUES FOR REDUCING FAT AND SALT IN SLOW COOKING

• Quite often fat is needed to brown meats or onions before cooking. Generally in slow cooking this whole step can be eliminated, so disregard the fat entirely.

• If fat is required to soften the vegetables, try substituting chicken stock or water to wilt vegetables.

• Trim excess fat off meats before cooking.

• For high-fat meats like hamburger and sausage; fry in a skillet and drain off fat before adding to your slow cooker.

• Skim fat off top of pot, if visible, or chill meat mixture; let fat solidify and skim fat off.

• Substitute ground turkey for ground beef to reduce fat.

• The best way to reduce salt in your recipe is to replace with spices or simply increase the quantity of spices already called for in the recipe, so salt is not so necessary.

• One method to reduce saltiness in a recipe is to add chunks of peeled potato, which will absorb the salt and remove the chunks before serving the dish.

• Another method to reduce saltiness is to add white pepper (not black). White pepper is more subtle and takes away from the salty flavor.

• Use low salt (or low sodium) canned foods and when the recipe calls for garlic salt or celery salt, use powdered garlic or celery instead (increasing the quantity somewhat).

TYPES OF SLOW COOKERS

Slow cookers come in many different shapes and sizes. They range from one solid unit, to separate liners with heating shells, to hot plates with pans on top. Technically, an electric skillet can be used as a slow cooker. Many new versions have deep frying attachments that can reach very high temperatures. A pot that separates from the heating unit for ease of cleaning and storage is a desirable feature.

Slow cooking can also be done in the oven using a casserole, Dutch oven or other ovenproof container with a tight-fitting lid so steam cannot readily escape.

Cook at LOW (200°F) by quadrupling the time for conventional stove top cooking. A stew which requires 2 to 2½ hours would be increased to 8 to 10 hours. Cook at HIGH (300°F) in the oven by doubling the time.

Be aware that using the oven to cook slowly does not save energy the way a slow cooker pot does and is therefore less economical.

Caring for your slow cooker should be done according to the manufacturer's instructions. Here are some of the surfaces that were used for testing:

Crockery lining. Usually made from glazed stoneware or earthenware, this should be washed (or at least soaked) soon after using. If the slow cooker has a separate liner, it usually can be put in a dishwasher (never immerse the outer electrical unit). Use nylon or plastic scrubbers to get out dried food or stains.

Aluminum lining. Using aluminum is not advised for health reasons and also limitations in cooking high acid foods. If you have one, wash it with soapy water, use nylon pads and always season with oil before using.

Porcelain or baked enamel lining. You need to be a little more cautious in handling this type. Be careful to cool completely before washing. Never use abrasive cleansers, only use nylon scrubbers and rinse very well before heating to avoid staining.

Glass or Corning Ware. This surface is ideal for slow cooking because it absorbs heat rapidly, withstands extreme temperatures and sudden temperatures, is easy to clean and holds heat a long time. Avoid using metal scouring pads.

Stainless steel. Stainless steel is good for heat retention and generally easy to clean. Avoid using steel wool to clean because it can scratch the surface.

Teflon coated. Use nylon or plastic utensils and definitely do not use anything other than nylon or plastic scrubbers. Teflon usually needs to be seasoned before using. If the surface discolors with time, use an appliance stain remover.

APPETIZERS

HONEY CHICKEN WINGS

This is a wonderful appetizer that can be kept warm and served from the slow cooker at a buffet.

3 lb. chicken wings
Salt and pepper, to taste
1 cup honey
3 Tbsp. ketchup

½ cup soy sauce
2 Tbsp. oil
1 clove garlic, minced
Sesame seeds for garnish, optional

Disjoint chicken wings and discard tips. Sprinkle wing parts with salt and pepper. Place honey, ketchup, soy sauce, oil, and garlic in the slow cooker. Stir until mixed well. Add seasoned chicken wings and stir. Set slow cooker on low and cook 5 to 6 hours. If desired, garnish with a sprinkling of sesame seeds.

HUMMUS DIP

MAKES ABOUT 2 CUPS

Hummus is a Middle Eastern vegetarian dip that has become very popular. I experimented using rehydrated beans versus slow-cooked beans and the results were far better with the slow cooker. For variety, add chopped cilantro.

¼ lb. dried garbanzo beans
Water to cover beans
1 Tbsp. olive oil
1 small onion, chopped
2 cloves garlic, minced

½ tsp. turmeric
2 Tbsp. chopped parsley
Salt, to taste
1–2 Tbsp. lemon juice, or more to taste

Rinse dried beans under cold running water. Place in the slow cooker and cover with water, making sure that you have at least 2 inches of water on top of beans. Set cooker on low and allow to cook for 8 to 10 hours. Drain beans, discard water, and rinse under cold water. Allow beans to drain well. Place in a food processor or blender and purée until about the consistency of mayonnaise. if mixture appears too coarse, add a little water. In a skillet, heat olive oil and sauté onion and garlic until soft and transparent. Add turmeric and cook an additional minute. Add this mixture to puréed beans in food processor and blend. Add parsley, salt, and lemon juice to taste.

HOT ARTICHOKE DIP
MAKES 7 TO 8 CUPS

This is an incredible dip that goes well with thick, mild-flavored crackers or slices of crusty French bread. Slow cookers are ideal for keeping food warm, especially at buffet parties.

2 jars (14¾ oz. each) marinated artichoke
   hearts, drained
1 cup mayonnaise, fat-free, if desired
1 cup sour cream, low-fat or fat-free, if desired

2 cups grated Parmesan cheese
1 cup chopped water chestnuts
¼ cup finely chopped green onion,
   or more to taste

Cut artichoke hearts into small pieces. Mix in mayonnaise, sour cream, Parmesan cheese, water chestnuts, and green onion. Place in the slow cooker on low for at least 1 hour or until thoroughly heated. Serve directly from slow cooker with crackers or sliced French bread.

CHILI CON QUESO (CHEESE DIP)

SERVES 8

The slow cooker is great for cheese dip because it can be used on a buffet table to keep the cheese warm.

2 Tbsp. butter
2 Tbsp. finely chopped onion
1–2 cloves garlic, minced

2 fresh tomatoes, peeled and seeded
4 oz. diced green chilies
2½ cups grated Monterey Jack or Cheddar cheese

Turn the slow cooker on high. Add butter, onion, and garlic, and sauté until onion is soft but not brown. Dice tomatoes and add to slow cooker with chilies and cheese. Heat on low for 1 hour or until cheese melts completely. Serve directly from slow cooker with corn chips or sliced French bread.

SPICY BEAN DIP

MAKES 4½ CUPS

This is a quick and easy vegetarian dip that can be "spiced up" with the addition of jalapeños.

2 cans (16 oz. each) refried beans*
1 pkg. (1¼ oz.) taco seasoning mix
½ cup finely chopped onion

2 cups shredded Monterey Jack or Cheddar cheese
Several drops Tabasco Sauce
Jalapeño peppers to taste, optional

Place refried beans, taco seasoning, onion, cheese, and Tabasco in the slow cooker and stir. If you wish to really add heat, carefully remove seeds and chop up jalapeño peppers (be careful not to touch your eyes or face) and stir into bean mixture to your personal taste. If mixture appears too thick, add a little water. Heat on low until mixture is hot and cheese is melted, approximately 1 hour. Serve directly from slow cooker with corn chips, sliced French bread or crackers.

NOTE: To reduce fat, use low-fat cheese and increase the seasoning slightly.

*vegetarian refried beans do not contain animal lard.

HOT BACON & CHEESE DIP

SERVES 8 TO 12

You can't go wrong with bacon and cheese. I particularly like to serve this with apple and pear slices or thin slices of French bread.

8 slices bacon, diced
8 oz. cream cheese, cubed
2 cups Monterey Jack cheese, shredded
6 Tbsp. half-and-half

1 tsp. Worcestershire sauce
¼ tsp. dry mustard
¼ tsp. onion salt
Dash of Tabasco Sauce

Fry finely diced bacon in a skillet until crispy; drain on paper towels and set aside. Place cream cheese, Monterey Jack cheese, half-and-half, Worcestershire sauce, mustard, onion salt, and Tabasco in the slow cooker. Set on low and allow cheese to melt slowly, stirring occasionally for approximately 1 hour. Taste and adjust seasonings. Just before guests arrive, stir in bacon and serve directly from slow cooker. If mixture becomes too thick, add more half-and-half to thin. If using apples and pears to accompany this dish, dip fruit slices in lemon juice to help prevent browning.

HOT HERBY MUSHROOMS

SERVES 12

For a change from baked mushrooms, try something that is healthy and easy to serve.

6 Tbsp. butter
1 large onion, chopped
2 tsp. basil
2 tsp. oregano
½ tsp. thyme

¼ cup lemon juice
½ cup sherry
¼ tsp. red pepper flakes
3 lb. mushrooms, washed and left whole

Turn the slow cooker on high. Melt butter; add onion and sauté until onion is limp. Turn cooker on low. Add spices, lemon juice, sherry, and pepper flakes; allow mixture to steep on low for 1 to 2 hours. Add mushrooms about 15 minutes before guests arrive. Use toothpicks or a slotted spoon to serve.

SOUPS

HUNGARIAN LAMB SOUP
SERVES 10 TO 12

Lamb soup is a delightful change from the old standard. It is important to use a good paprika. I prefer the sweet Hungarian variety.

¼ cup butter
2 medium onions, chopped
2 lb. lamb shoulder
1 Tbsp. Hungarian paprika
2 qt. beef stock
2 bay leaves

Salt and pepper, to taste
2–3 potatoes, peeled and cubed
½ cup sliced fresh green beans
1 Tbsp. flour
1 cup sour cream

In a skillet, melt butter and add onions. While onions are sautéing, trim lamb of fat and cut into ½-inch cubes. Add lamb to skillet and brown. Stir in paprika and heat for 1 minute. Pour skillet ingredients into the slow cooker with stock, bay leaves, salt, and pepper. Set cooker on low and cook for 6 to 7 hours. Add potatoes and green beans and cook on low for 1 hour more, or until the potatoes are fork tender. Half an hour before serving, mix flour with sour cream. Gently stir mixture into soup and allow to heat before serving. Taste and adjust seasonings.

SPLIT PEA & HAM SOUP
SERVES 8 TO 10

This soup is nutritious and filling. The addition of a smoked ham shank gives it a slightly smoky flavor.

4 slices bacon, diced
1½ medium onions, chopped
2 carrots, diced
2 stalks celery, diced
1 lb. dried split peas
1 smoked ham shank
2 bay leaves

3 qt. water
¼–½ tsp. cayenne pepper
Salt and pepper, to taste
1 cup cooked ham, diced
2 slices bacon, fried and crumbled,
  optional for garnish

In a skillet, fry bacon until crisp; remove and drain on paper towels. Sauté onions, carrots, and celery in bacon fat for 5 minutes. Place bacon, sautéed vegetables, peas, ham shank, bay leaves, water, cayenne pepper, salt, and pepper in the slow cooker. Set cooker on low and cook for 8 to 9 hours or until peas are soft. If you wish to have a smooth texture, purée soup in a food processor or blender and return to slow cooker. Add diced ham before serving and stir until heated through. Taste and adjust seasonings. If desired, add bacon garnish.

PROVENÇAL VEGETABLE SOUP
SERVES 8

Garlic paste makes this different from traditional vegetable soup.

1 medium onion, diced
1 leek, diced
2 cups fresh green beans
2 cups peeled, diced potatoes
2 cups diced carrots
2 cups diced tomatoes
2½ qt. water
Salt and pepper, to taste
2 diced zucchini

½ lb. mushrooms, sliced
3 cloves garlic
2 Tbsp. chopped fresh basil or 2 tsp. dried basil
Salt, to taste
1 can (6 oz.) tomato paste
¼ cup grated Parmesan cheese
¼ cup olive oil
Grated Parmesan cheese or chopped parsley
    for garnish

In the slow cooker, place onion, leek, green beans, potatoes, carrots, tomatoes, and water. Cook on low for 3 hours. Add salt, pepper, zucchini, and mushrooms; cook 1 hour longer. With a mortar and pestle or a wooden spoon, crush garlic and mix in chopped basil and salt until a paste is formed. To this paste, add tomato paste, Parmesan cheese, and olive oil and mix well. Add a bit of soup to paste; then stir paste into soup. Blend well and allow to heat for 15 minutes before serving. Taste and adjust seasonings. Garnish with Parmesan cheese or parsley.

VICHYSSOISE

SERVES 6 TO 8

This is a classic leek and potato soup that has been adapted to the slow cooker. Traditionally this soup is served cold but it can be served hot.

2 lb. leeks
2 lb. potatoes
7 cups chicken stock
2¼ cups milk

1½ cups cream
Salt and pepper, to taste
Fresh chives for garnish

Trim off tough green leaves from leeks; split bulbs open and carefully wash out dirt between layers. Thinly slice leeks. Peel potatoes and dice. Place leeks, potatoes, and chicken stock in the slow cooker; set on low and cook for 3 to 4 hours or until vegetables are tender. Purée entire mixture in a food processor or blender. Return mixture to slow cooker and add milk, cream, salt, and pepper. Cook on low until mixture is heated through. Taste and adjust seasoning. If serving chilled, allow soup to come to room temperature and then refrigerate. Garnish with fresh chives and ground pepper.

BEEF VEGETABLE BARLEY SOUP
SERVES 10 TO 12

This is an easy recipe with a secret ingredient, oatmeal, that gives it body and a special flavor.

1 lb. beef stew meat, cut into 1-inch cubes
1 large beef knuckle bone, cut in half
1 large onion, diced
3 stalks celery, coarsely chopped
2 whole cloves garlic, peeled
1 tsp. salt
1 medium rutabaga, peeled, cut into ½-inch cubes

3 qt. water
8 carrots, cut into 1-inch pieces
2 parsnips, peeled, cut into ½-inch pieces
3 beef bouillon cubes
1 cup barley
½ cup oatmeal
Salt and pepper, to taste

Place stew meat, knuckle bone, onion, celery, garlic, salt, rutabaga, and water in the slow cooker. Set on low and cook for 7 to 8 hours. Remove knuckle bone and strip off any meat and marrow. Discard bone. Add meat and marrow to slow cooker. Add carrots, parsnips, and bouillon cubes and cook on low for 2 hours. Add barley and oatmeal and cook for 1 to 2 hours. Taste and add salt and pepper, if desired. Soup is done when vegetables are tender.

BLACK BEAN SOUP
SERVES 6

Black beans have become very popular lately. They are healthy and have great flavor. Keep in mind that the red pepper really spices up this recipe, so you may want to be cautious about the size of the pepper or possibly eliminate it. This soup needs a little color, so I suggest using either one or several of the suggested garnishes.

2 cups dried black beans
6–8 cups chicken, beef or vegetable broth
1 large onion, chopped
4 cloves garlic, crushed
1 whole dried red serrano pepper
2 tsp. cumin
2 tsp. oregano
½ tsp. cinnamon

2 bay leaves
2 tsp. salt
2–3 carrots, sliced
3 stalks celery, sliced
Sour cream, chopped tomatoes, roasted red pepper sauce, minced parsley and/or minced cilantro for garnish, optional

Rinse beans and place in the slow cooker. Add broth. Use 6 cups for thick soup or 8 cups for thinner soup. Stir in remaining ingredients and cover. Set on low and cook for 9 to 10 hours. Add desired garnishes and serve.

NOTE: For a higher protein meal, add a ham hock at the start of cooking period and shred meat from bone at end or add cubed, cooked ham just before serving.

BEST-EVER CHICKEN STOCK

MAKES 1 GALLON

Chicken stock is the basis for many soups and sauces and can be used in place of butter or oil to add flavor without fat when frying vegetables. Adding onion skins to the stock will give it extra flavor and a darker color.

2 lb. chicken parts
1 lb. veal bones
1 gal. cold water
4 carrots, diced
2 medium onions, diced
½ tsp. whole cloves
3 stalks celery, diced
1 Tbsp. salt

1 tsp. black peppercorns
Handful parsley stems, not leaves
2 bay leaves
1 rosemary sprig or 1 tsp. dried
1 thyme sprig or 1 tsp. dried
Few blades mace, or dash nutmeg
2 whole cloves garlic, peeled

Place chicken parts and veal bones in the slow cooker and cover with water. Turn slow cooker on high and as scum rises to top, remove it with a slotted spoon. After scum ceases to form, turn slow cooker on low and add remaining ingredients. If fresh rosemary and thyme are not available, wrap dried rosemary and thyme in cheesecloth; place in pot and remove at end of cooking. Cook for 6 hours; strain broth; taste and adjust seasonings. When cool, refrigerate until ready to use.

VEGETARIAN ENTRÉES

FALAFEL (CHICKPEA BURGERS)

SERVES 6

Falafel is a Middle Eastern vegetarian dish made from garbanzo beans which are formed into little patties and quickly fried. They are good served in pita bread with hummus and either sprouts or tabbouleh salad. Traditionally, this is served with tahini (sesame paste) dip.

½ lb. dried garbanzo beans or fava beans
Water to cover
1 Tbsp. chopped cilantro
1 Tbsp. chopped parsley
4 green onions, chopped
2 cloves garlic, minced

½–1 tsp. cumin
Pinch baking soda
Salt and pepper, to taste
Water to moisten, optional
Olive oil for frying

Rinse dried beans under running water; place in the slow cooker and cover with water (at least 2 inches over top of beans). Cook on low for 8 to 10 hours. Pour off water, rinse under cold water and allow to drain. Place cooked beans in a food processor or blender and purée until slightly grainy. Add cilantro, parsley, onions, garlic, cumin, soda, salt, and pepper. Blend until just mixed. Taste mixture and adjust seasonings. Moisten your hands with water and form mixture into small patties. If mixture seems too dry to form proper patties, add a small amount of water. Heat olive oil in a skillet and fry patties until brown on both sides.

BALSAMIC VINAIGRETTE

1 cup olive oil
⅓ cup balsamic vinegar
1 tsp. Dijon mustard
1–2 tsp. sugar
Salt and pepper, to taste

Mix all ingredients together in a food processor or blender. Taste and add additional seasonings to your personal taste.

KAMUT VEGETABLE SALAD

SERVES 6 TO 8

This healthy, chewy grain complements vegetables perfectly.

1 cup whole grain kamut
3 cups water
½ tsp. salt
1 cup chopped celery
1 cup chopped red cabbage

½ cup diced red bell peppers
¼ cup diced green onions
¼ cup diced red onion
2–4 Tbsp. chopped cilantro, to taste

Place kamut, water, and salt in the slow cooker. Set on low and cook 8 to 9 hours. Allow grains to cool thoroughly. Mix in celery, cabbage, peppers, red and green onions, and cilantro. Make vinaigrette recipe on left and add enough vinaigrette to moisten.

SIMPLE TOMATO SAUCE

SERVES 6

Try this recipe for a quick, tasty sauce that takes just minutes to prepare. Serve over pasta or spaghetti squash with a sprinkling of Parmesan for a good vegetarian meal.

2 Tbsp. olive oil
1 large onion, chopped
4–5 cups canned plum tomatoes, undrained
1 can (6 oz.) tomato paste

2 tsp. basil
2 tsp. oregano
2 tsp. sugar
Salt and pepper, to taste

Turn the slow cooker on high; add oil and onion. Allow onion to soften and wilt slightly. Set cooker on low, add remaining ingredients and cook for 4 to 6 hours. Taste and season to your personal preference before serving.

BLACK BEAN CHILI

SERVES 6 TO 8

Ideal for cold, autumn or winter days, black beans have great flavor and are low-fat. If served with rice or potatoes, this makes a healthy, complete protein meal.

1 cup dried black beans
4 cups water
½ tsp. cumin seeds
⅛ tsp. cayenne pepper
½ tsp. paprika
1 medium onion, chopped
3 cloves garlic, mashed
1 tsp. dry mustard

1 tsp. chili powder
2 large tomatoes, preferably plum variety
2 Tbsp. tomato paste
½ red bell pepper, chopped
1 can (4 oz.) diced green chilies
Salt, to taste
6 oz. low-fat cheese, shredded
Cilantro leaves for garnish

Soak beans in water overnight. Drain and discard water. Place beans and water in the slow cooker and set on high. Cook until tender, about 6 hours. The next step is not necessary, but I find that it really intensifies the flavor. Heat a skillet on medium and toast cumin seeds until they begin to pop, about 2 to 3 minutes. Add cayenne pepper and paprika and cook for 1 minute. (Note: This is extremely fragrant so have the fan running.) Add the toasted spices and onion to the cooked beans in the slow cooker. Next mix the mashed garlic with dry mustard and add them to the beans. Add chili powder. Seed and chop tomatoes and add to pot with tomato paste, bell pepper, and green chilies. Set cooker on low and allow to cook for 3 to 4 hours. Taste and add salt, if desired. Before serving, add shredded cheese and cilantro leaves.

MARINATED GARBANZO BEAN SALAD

SERVES 6

Instead of the same old three-bean salad, try something new. This salad can be served warm or cold.

3 cups dried garbanzo beans
Water to cover
1 Tbsp. olive oil
2 Tbsp. vegetable stock or chicken stock
½ cup chopped onion

1 Tbsp. thyme
½ red bell pepper, chopped
½ cup currants or raisins
2 Tbsp. balsamic vinegar

In the slow cooker, cover dried beans with water (at least 2 inches above beans). Cook on low for 8 hours. Drain beans; discard water and measure out 3 cups. (If there are extra beans, add to a tossed salad or use to make hummus dip.) Place oil and 1 tablespoon vegetable stock in a skillet. Add onion and thyme; cook on medium until onion is soft and beginning to turn brown, about 10 minutes. Add remaining tablespoon. vegetable stock and pepper; stir-fry for several minutes. Add currants and cooked beans; cook for 5 minutes. Remove mixture from heat, pour into a bowl and let cool. Add vinegar and mix well. Taste and add more seasonings or vinegar to taste.

MEAT & POULTRY ENTRÉES

BEER STEW
SERVES 6

This is a basic beef stew with a twist—beer. It adds a unique flavor and helps tenderize the meat.

2½ lb. beef stew meat or chuck roast
1 large onion, chopped
2 cloves garlic, minced
4–5 carrots, cut into chunks
2–3 stalks celery, cut into slices
16 oz. beer
2½ tsp. salt

½ tsp. pepper
1½ tsp. oregano
2 Tbsp. tomato paste
3–4 Tbsp. melted butter
⅓ cup flour
Chopped parsley for garnish, optional

Cut beef into 1-inch squares. Place beef, onion, garlic, carrots, celery, beer, salt, pepper, oregano, and tomato paste in the slow cooker. Set cooker on low and cook for 8 to 10 hours. Mix melted butter with flour until a smooth, thick paste is formed and stir into stew. Taste stew and adjust seasonings to your personal preference. Turn slow cooker on high and allow mixture to thicken before serving. Garnish with chopped parsley.

NOTE: If you like potatoes in your stew, add canned potatoes (cut into chunks) just before serving.

COLORADO CHILI

SERVES 4 TO 6

This chili is made with large red Colorado chili peppers which are ground into a paste and added to cooked meat. Great with beans.

2 lb. lean beef or pork

2 cups water

Salt, to taste

8 large dried red Colorado chili peppers

Warm water to cover chili peppers

2 cloves garlic, peeled

1 tsp. oregano

¼ cup oil, or less if desired

2 Tbsp. flour

Salt, to taste

Pinch cumin, or to taste

Cut beef or pork into cubes and place in the slow cooker with water and salt. Cook on high for 1 to 2 hours. Drain meat and reserve liquid. While meat is cooking, cover peppers with warm water and allow to soak for 20 to 30 minutes. Drain peppers and reserve liquid. Cut peppers open and remove seeds. Purée peppers, garlic, and oregano in a food processor or blender to consistency of paste. Add 1 cup reserved meat liquid and ½ cup reserved liquid from chili peppers to paste. Stir until mixed well. In a skillet, heat oil; stir in flour and add chili mixture, salt, and cumin and cook for 5 minutes. Add chili mixture to slow cooker with meat and set on low. Cook for 4 to 6 hours. Taste and adjust seasonings. Before serving, garnish with chopped onions.

OLIVE SPAGHETTI SAUCE

SERVES 8 TO 10

When the "old red spaghetti sauce" gets boring, try something new. This sauce is made with green olives, but, if you don't like them, you can substitute black olives.

1 lb. lean ground beef
½ lb. ground veal
¼ lb. Italian sausage
1 cup water
1 tsp. salt
⅛ tsp. pepper
1 can (28 oz.) tomatoes, chopped
12 oz. tomato paste
1½ cups Burgundy wine
1 cup chopped onion

¾ cup chopped green bell pepper
3 cloves garlic, crushed
2 tsp. sugar
½ tsp. chili powder
1½ tsp. Worcestershire sauce
3 bay leaves
1 cup sliced mushrooms, fresh or canned
½ cup sliced stuffed green olives
Grated Parmesan cheese

In a heavy skillet, brown beef, veal, and sausage. Drain off fat. Put browned meat, water, salt, pepper, tomatoes, tomato paste, Burgundy, onion, peppers, garlic, sugar, chili powder, Worcestershire sauce, bay leaves, and fresh mushrooms (not canned) in the slow cooker. Cook on low for 8 hours. About half an hour before serving, add olives to cooker. Add canned mushrooms if you are using them. Cook half an hour longer. Serve over pasta and sprinkle with Parmesan.

WINE STEW

SERVES 6

Stew does not have to be limited to carrots and potatoes in gravy. Try something new—mixing meats, using wine and serving with rice.

2½ lb. top sirloin
2 Tbsp. butter or bacon fat
½ lb. ham, preferably Westphalian
2 large onions, diced
½ cup stuffed green olives, halved
2–3 cloves garlic, minced
¾ tsp. thyme
½ cup raisins

3 cups red wine
2 tsp. pepper
1 tsp. salt, or to taste
¼ cup brandy
¾ cup cream
¼ cup flour
½ cup water

Cut sirloin into 2-inch pieces. In a skillet, heat butter on high and brown beef cubes. Add ham and onions; stir until slightly brown. Transfer mixture to the slow cooker and set on low. Add olives, garlic, thyme, raisins, and wine. Cook for 7 to 8 hours. Add pepper, salt, brandy, and cream; cook 1 hour longer. Remove meat from cooker and keep warm. Turn cooker on high; mix flour with water and add to cooker. Stir until mixture begins to thicken. If you desire a thicker sauce, add more flour-water mixture. Taste and adjust seasonings. Pour sauce over meat and serve.

PORK ADOBO

SERVES 6 TO 8

This is a braised pork dish common in the Philippines. Serve with white rice or more healthful brown rice.

2½ lb. lean pork
Salt to taste
¼ cup flour
1 Tbsp. oil
2–3 cloves garlic, minced
2 medium onions, quartered

2 bay leaves
4 Tbsp. cider vinegar
1 Tbsp. soy sauce
¼ cup water
1 tsp. sugar, optional
Beaten, fried egg for garnish, optional

Cut fat off pork and cut into 1½-inch cubes. Mix salt and flour together and coat pork cubes. Heat oil in a skillet and fry pork until brown. Add garlic and cook 1 minute. Add onions and bay leaves and cook until onions begin to brown. Transfer ingredients to the slow cooker. Set cooker on low; add remaining ingredients except sugar and egg. Cook for 6 to 8 hours or until pork is tender. Taste and adjust seasonings. Add sugar, if desired. Typically, the garnish is an egg which has been beaten, fried and cut into thin strips.

SPECIAL BOLOGNESE SAUCE
SERVES 12

My friend, Sam, brought me a sample of a sauce he had obtained in his travels and asked me to try to duplicate it. The secret ingredients that made this sauce unique were thyme and Dijon mustard, which, I'm sure, aren't normal Italian flavors! Give it a try—you might be pleasantly surprised.

1½ lb. lean ground beef
1 cup chopped onion
2 carrots, chopped
2 stalks celery, chopped
5 cups chopped, canned tomatoes
1 cup white wine
1½ tsp. salt
½ tsp. pepper

4 cloves garlic, minced
2 tsp. oregano
2 tsp. basil
1 tsp. rosemary
½ tsp. anise seeds
1 Tbsp. thyme
1½ Tbsp. Dijon mustard
1 Tbsp. sugar, or to taste

In a skillet, brown beef and onion until no red remains in meat and beef is crumbled. Drain off excess fat. Place browned beef and onion in the slow cooker and stir in remaining ingredients. Cover and set cooker on low for 6 to 8 hours. Taste and adjust seasonings. Serve over hot pasta.

INCREDIBLE CHILI

SERVES 12

This is the " true" chili made the old-fashioned way. It's worth the effort.

½ lb. bacon, diced
3 medium onions, minced
1½ lb. pork loin
1½ lb. sirloin tip
1½ lb. ground chuck (chili grind)
2 cans (15 oz. each) tomato sauce
18 oz. beer
3 cloves garlic, minced

1 jalapeño pepper, seeded and minced
2 Tbsp. ground cumin
½ tsp. oregano
2–3 Tbsp. mild chili powder
Salt and pepper, to taste
2 cups dried pinto beans, optional
Grated cheese, optional

In a skillet, fry bacon until brown. Drain and place in the slow cooker. Remove all but a small amount of fat from skillet and sauté onions until slightly brown. Place onions in slow cooker. Cut pork loin and sirloin tip into ¼-inch dice and brown with ground chuck in skillet. Drain off fat and add meat to slow cooker. Add remaining ingredients except cheese. If you choose to use pinto beans, soak in water overnight, discard water, add beans to slow cooker and stir. Set cooker on low and cook for 6 to 8 hours. Meat should be very tender. Taste and adjust seasonings. If desired, sprinkle with cheese before serving.

SWEET & SOUR BEEF
SERVES 4 TO 6

Sweet-and-sour is a popular flavor usually reserved for pork or chicken. This is a delicious beef version that is good served over rice or noodles.

2 lb. boneless chuck
⅓ cup flour
1 tsp. salt
¼ tsp. black pepper
1 Tbsp. butter
1 Tbsp. olive oil
1 large onion, chopped
½ cup ketchup

¼ cup brown sugar
¼ cup red wine vinegar
1 Tbsp. Worcestershire sauce
1 cup water
1 tsp. salt
Pepper to taste, optional
4 – 6 carrots, julienned

Cut beef into 1-inch cubes. Mix together flour, salt and pepper and dredge cubes in mixture. In a skillet, heat butter and olive oil and brown beef cubes. Place browned beef in the slow cooker and set on low. Add remaining ingredients except carrots. Cook for 8 to 9 hours or until meat is tender. Add carrots and cook 1½ to 2 hours longer. Taste, adjust seasonings and serve.

SAUSAGE & BAKED BEANS

SERVES 9

Even though this recipe uses canned beans, adding delicious ingredients and cooking on low for a long time really enhances the flavor.

1 lb. ground pork sausage
4 – 5 slices bacon, diced
1 large onion, chopped
1 stalk celery, chopped
1 can (28 oz.) baked beans
¾ tsp. basil
1 Tbsp. chopped parsley

2 Tbsp. chutney
2 Tbsp. soy sauce
2 Tbsp. cider or red wine vinegar
1 can (15 oz.) tomatoes
1 tsp. salt
½ cup molasses

Brown sausage and bacon in a skillet and drain off fat. Place browned meats in the slow cooker with remaining ingredients. Set cooker on low and cook for 6 hours. Check the quantity of liquid; if it seems excessive, pour a little off and reserve for later. Stir and continue cooking an additional 6 hours. Check to determine if you need to add some reserved liquid. Taste and adjust seasonings.

SOUTH AMERICAN BRAISED BEEF

SERVES 4

Slow cooking can turn even a round steak into a cut-with-a-fork tender piece of meat. I usually shred the meat and, with a little sauce, use it to fill tortillas.

2 cloves garlic, minced	1 medium onion, chopped
2 lb. beef round steak	1 cup chopped carrots
1 tsp. salt	1 tsp. marjoram
¼ tsp. pepper	½ cup beef broth
2 Tbsp. lime or lemon juice	1 can (14½ oz.) peeled tomatoes

Spread minced garlic on round steak and sprinkle with salt, pepper, and lime juice. Place in the slow cooker and add remaining ingredients. Set cooker on low and cook for approximately 8 hours. Meat should be fork tender and shred easily. If not, return to pot and cook additional time. Taste and add extra seasonings if desired.

BURGUNDY BEEF

SERVES 8

Whenever you cook with wine, use a wine you would gladly drink. Don't waste the recipe with cheap wine. Use a good Burgundy in this recipe and you'll reap the rewards. Serve this with gnocchi, noodles, rice or potatoes.

4 Tbsp. butter

4 Tbsp. olive oil

1 can (1¼ lb.) small white onions

4 lb. chuck, cut into 2-inch cubes

¼ cup flour

1 tsp. Kitchen Bouquet

1 Tbsp. tomato paste

3 cups Burgundy wine

¼ tsp. pepper

3 bay leaves

½ tsp. thyme

½ tsp. marjoram

1 tbs. chopped fresh parsley

¾ lb. fresh or canned mushrooms

In a skillet, heat butter and oil and sauté onions until brown. Remove from skillet and place in the slow cooker. In the same skillet, brown meat cubes on all sides and then add them to the slow cooker. Discard all but 1 tablespoon of fat from the skillet and add flour, Kitchen Bouquet, and tomato paste and stir until smooth. Gradually stir in Burgundy wine. Add mixture to the slow cooker with pepper, bay leaves, thyme, marjoram, parsley, and mushrooms. Set cooker on low; cook 8 to 9 hours. Taste and add salt, if desired.

GROUND LAMB & ONION CURRY

SERVES 4

A great dish to have when you crave something spicy and different.

3 Tbsp. oil
2 large onions, thinly sliced
1 Tbsp. peeled, chopped fresh ginger
2 cloves garlic, minced
1 tsp. salt
1 lb. ground lamb
2–3 tsp. curry powder
¼ tsp. cinnamon
½ tsp. turmeric

½ tsp. coriander powder
½ tsp. cumin
Dash Tabasco Sauce or red pepper
  flakes pepper, to taste
4 cups tomatoes, peeled, seeded
  and chopped
2 Tbsp. plain yogurt
Chopped cilantro for garnish

Heat oil in a skillet and add onions, ginger, garlic, and salt. Sauté until onions begin to brown. Add lamb and cook until no longer pink. Drain grease from meat mixture. Add curry powder, cinnamon, turmeric, coriander, cumin, Tabasco, and pepper. Stir for several minutes to release flavor of spices. Transfer ingredients to the slow cooker and set temperature to low for 1 to 2 hours. Add tomatoes and yogurt to lamb mixture and cook half an hour longer. Taste and adjust seasonings. Serve over rice and garnish liberally with chopped cilantro.

CRANBERRY CHICKEN

SERVES 4

Cranberries add a slightly tangy flavor to slow-cooked chicken dishes. The berries tend to dissolve so they are not noticeable. With the addition of a little brown sugar, the chicken takes on a slightly sweet-and-sour taste. This dish is good served with brown rice.

1 broiler chicken
¾ cup chopped onion
1 cup fresh cranberries
1 tsp. salt
¼ tsp. cinnamon
¼ tsp. ginger

1 tsp. grated orange rind
1 cup orange juice
3 Tbsp. melted butter
3 Tbsp. flour
2–3 Tbsp. brown sugar, optional

Cut chicken into quarters and remove skin. Place in the slow cooker with onion, cranberries, salt, cinnamon, ginger, orange rind, and orange juice. Cover and cook on low for 5 to 6 hours. Remove chicken from pot and separate meat from bone; set aside. Mix butter and flour together to form a thick paste. Stir paste into liquid in pot and turn on high to thicken sauce. Add reserved chicken meat and taste. Add brown sugar and any additional seasonings to suit your taste.

CHICKEN CURRY

SERVES 8

Ideally, curries should be accompanied with several condiments like chutney, chopped green onions, raisins, chopped nuts, etc. Serve this dish with rice.

6 whole chicken breasts
Water to cover
½ tsp. peppercorns
1 tsp. salt
2 stalks celery, chopped
½ cup butter
1 Tbsp. oil
2 medium onions, chopped
3 cloves garlic, minced

2 stalks celery, chopped
3 Tbsp. chopped parsley
1 cucumber, chopped, preferably English variety
2 apples, cored, peeled and chopped, preferably Golden Delicious
¼ cup flour
1 tsp. nutmeg

1 tsp. dry mustard
3 Tbsp. curry powder, or to taste
2 cups chicken broth
2 cups cream
1 cup coconut milk
1½ tsp. salt
1 Tbsp. lemon juice

Split chicken breasts; place in the slow cooker. Add water, peppercorns, salt, and celery. Set on low and cook 5 to 6 hours or until chicken is tender. Remove chicken and discard liquid. Debone chicken and cut meat into dice or shred. Set aside. Turn slow cooker on high; heat butter and oil; add onions, garlic, celery, parsley, cucumber, and apples. Sauté until tender, stirring frequently. Stir in flour, nutmeg, mustard, and curry powder; cook 5 minutes longer. Add chicken broth, cream, coconut milk, and salt. Allow mixture to heat up, turn cooker to low and allow sauce to cook for 2 to 3 hours. Press sauce through a sieve. Add lemon juice; taste and adjust seasonings. Transfer chicken to slow cooker and cover with sauce. Heat on low until ready to serve.

CHICKEN PASTA SALAD

SERVES 6 TO 8

Pasta and succulent poached chicken are very tasty together. This salad stores well and is great for picnics.

3 whole chicken breasts
Water to cover
1 stalk celery, chopped
½ large onion, chopped
½ tsp. salt
A few peppercorns
6 oz. dried pasta of choice
½ cup oil
1 Tbsp. sesame oil

⅓ cup light soy sauce
⅓ cup rice vinegar
3 Tbsp. sugar
¼ tsp. pepper
½ tsp. ground ginger
¼ cup chopped parsley
⅓ cup sliced green onions
6 cups fresh spinach
¼ cup toasted sesame seeds

Cut chicken breasts in half and place in the slow cooker. Cover with water and add celery, onion, salt, and peppercorns. Set on low and cook 5 to 6 hours. When chicken is cooked thoroughly, remove and let cool. Cut into chunks or shred. Cook dried pasta according to package directions until just barely tender (al dente); drain and set aside to cool. In a separate bowl, combine oils, soy sauce, vinegar, sugar, pepper, and ginger. Add to chicken and pasta and let marinate for at least 1 hour. Toss in parsley, onions, spinach, and sesame seeds. Taste and adjust seasonings and serve.

CHUTNEY CHICKEN SALAD

SERVES 6

Poaching chicken slowly gives it a succulent quality perfect for salads.

4–5 full chicken breasts
2 bay leaves
1 tsp. salt
½ tsp. peppercorns
½ medium onion, coarsely chopped
2 stalks celery, chopped
Water to cover
1 cup mayonnaise
½ cup chopped chutney

1 tsp. curry powder
2 tsp. grated lemon or lime peel
¼ cup lemon or lime juice
½ tsp. salt
1½ cups canned pineapple chunks
½ cup sliced green onions
1½ cups chopped celery
½ cup slivered toasted almonds

Cut chicken breasts in half and place in the slow cooker with bay leaves, salt, peppercorns, onion, and celery. Cover with water. Set cooker on low and cook for 4 to 6 hours. Take out a chicken piece and cut it in half to make sure chicken is cooked thoroughly. Remove chicken from pot and cool. If you wish, strain vegetables from liquid and save for future use. Dice chicken to make approximately 4 cups chicken meat. Combine mayonnaise, chutney, curry, lemon peel, lemon juice, and salt. Toss with chicken; add remaining ingredients except almonds. Chill well. When ready to serve, sprinkle with almonds.

STUFFED CHICKEN ROLLS

SERVES 6

This is a low-fat, easy meal that looks and tastes like you spent hours in the kitchen. Serve this with a rice pilaf or simple mashed potatoes.

3 whole chicken breasts	¼ tsp. ground rosemary
6 thin slices prosciutto or ham	¼ cup grated Parmesan cheese
6 thin slices low-fat Swiss cheese	2 tsp. cornstarch
Flour to coat chicken	1 Tbsp. water
½ lb. fresh sliced mushrooms	1 tsp. Kitchen Bouquet
½ cup chicken stock	Salt and pepper, to taste
½ cup white wine or Marsala wine	1 tsp. sugar, optional

Skin and bone chicken breasts and cut in half. Place chicken pieces between 2 pieces of waxed paper and pound until slightly flattened. Place 1 slice of prosciutto and 1 slice of cheese on each breast and roll up. Secure with a toothpick and roll in flour. Put mushrooms in the slow cooker and place chicken rolls on top of mushrooms. In a separate bowl, mix chicken stock, wine, and rosemary together; pour over chicken. Sprinkle with Parmesan cheese. Set slow cooker on low and cook for 6 hours. Just before serving, mix cornstarch, water and Kitchen Bouquet together. Remove chicken; add cornstanch mixture and stir until thickened. Add salt, pepper, and sugar, if desired. Pour sauce over chicken and serve.

DESSERTS

HOT CHOCOLATE PUDDING
SERVES 8

This is a fudgy, rich chocolate pudding that can be mixed right in the slow cooker. If desired, you can serve with a dollop of whipped cream, a scoop of vanilla ice cream or frozen yogurt.

1½ cups flour
1 cup sugar
3 Tbsp. unsweetened cocoa powder
1 Tbsp. baking powder
¾ tsp. salt
¾ cup milk
3 Tbsp. melted butter
1 tsp. vanilla

¾ cup packed brown sugar
⅓ cup sugar
¼ cup unsweetened cocoa powder
¼ tsp. salt
1½ tsp. vanilla
1½ cups boiling water
3 Tbsp. whipped cream
Cocoa powder, for garnish

Mix flour, sugar, cocoa, baking powder, and salt together in the slow cooker. Next add the milk, butter, and vanilla and stir until blended. In a separate bowl, mix together the sugars, cocoa, salt, and vanilla. Sprinkle on top of the mixture in the slow cooker without stirring. Pour boiling water on top. Do not mix.
Set slow cooker on low and cook for 3 hours. Just before serving, add whipped cream and a sprinkling sof cocoa powder.

APPLE INDIAN PUDDING

SERVES 8

Indian pudding is an old-fashioned cornmeal pudding that is strongly flavored with molasses. Apples add texture and moistness and give this dessert real substance. This is a great finale to a traditional meat and potatoes meal.

2 cups milk

⅓ cup cornmeal

2 cups sliced apples, preferably Golden Delicious

¾ cup molasses

¼ cup melted butter

1 tsp. salt

1 tsp. ginger

½ tsp. cinnamon

3 Tbsp. sugar

1 beaten egg

½ cup light or dark raisins

Whipped cream for garnish

Bring milk to a boil in a saucepan and add cornmeal. Place mixture in the slow cooker and add remaining ingredients. Amount of sugar varies depending on the type of apples used. Set slow cooker on low and cook for 4 to 5 hours. Allow pudding to cool to room temperature before serving as it will thicken as it cools. Since pudding is a dark brown color, I would suggest serving it with a dollop of whipped cream, ice cream or frozen yogurt.

BREAD PUDDING

SERVES 6 TO 8

This easy-to-make bread pudding reminds me of the kind of homey food my grandmother used to make on cold, wintry days.

4 cups toasted bread cubes
2½ cups scalded milk
2 eggs
¾ cup sugar
¼ tsp. cinnamon
Pinch nutmeg

Pinch salt
1 tsp. vanilla
2 Tbsp. melted butter
½ cup raisins, optional
Whipped cream for garnish

Put bread cubes in the slow cooker. In a separate container, mix scalded milk, eggs, sugar, cinnamon, nutmeg, salt, vanilla, and melted butter. Pour mixture over bread cubes and add raisins, if desired. With the back of a spoon, gently press all bread cubes into milk mixture to make sure liquid is absorbed. Avoid stirring mixture so bread does not disintegrate. Set cooker on low and cook for 5 to 6 hours. Serve warm with a dollop of whipped cream, if desired.

PINEAPPLE BREAD PUDDING
SERVES 8 TO 10

My friend, Joan, brought this recipe to a party and the guests raved, so I adapted the recipe for the slow cooker with a few minor changes. Thanks, Joan!

1 cup softened butter
2 cups sugar
1 tsp. cinnamon
8 eggs

2 cans (13½ oz. each) crushed pineapple
5 cups toasted bread cubes
½ cup chopped toasted pecans
Whipped cream for garnish

In a bowl, beat butter, sugar, and cinnamon until well mixed. Add eggs and beat on high until mixture is light and fluffy. Drain pineapple well. Reserve juice for later use. Fold pineapple and bread cubes into creamed mixture. Pour batter into the slow cooker; set cooker on low for 6 to 7 hours. Before serving, sprinkle pecans on top of pudding and serve warm with a dollop of whipped cream. Serve warm.

RASPBERRY SAUCE

1 pkg. (10 oz.) frozen raspberries
½ cup raspberry jam
Few drops lemon juice
Sugar, optional
1 Tbsp. raspberry liqueur, optional

Defrost raspberries. Place raspberries, raspberry jam and lemon juice into a food processor or blender. Purée until smooth; taste and add sugar, if desired. Strain through a sieve to remove seeds. Add raspberry liqueur, if desired. Drizzle sauce over warm Raspberry Bread Pudding, recipe on right.

RASPBERRY BREAD PUDDING

SERVES 8

This is a delightful change from the standard bread pudding. Don't limit yourself to raspberries—consider using blackberries, Marion berries, loganberries, etc., for a fruity, warm winter treat.

5 cups toasted bread cubes
2½ cups scalded milk
2 eggs
2 egg yolks
1 cup sugar
1 tsp. almond extract
2 Tbsp. melted butter
12 oz. fresh or frozen raspberries
Whipped cream for garnish

Place toasted bread cubes in the slow cooker. In a separate bowl, mix scalded milk, eggs, egg yolks, sugar, almond extract, and melted butter together. Defrost berries; drain off any excess juice and mix berries with bread cubes. Pour milk mixture on top and gently press bread into milk mixture with the back of a spoon. Do not stir mixture. Set slow cooker on low and cook for 4 to 6 hours. Serve warm with a dollop of whipped cream or drizzle with Raspberry Sauce, recipe on left.

APPLE DATE PUDDING

SERVES 8

This delicious, easy-to-fix, warm dessert can be topped with whipped cream or ice cream.

4 –5 apples, peeled, cored and diced
¾ cup sugar, or less, to taste
½ cup chopped dates
½ cup toasted, chopped pecans
2 Tbsp. flour

1 tsp. baking powder
⅛ tsp. salt
¼ tsp. nutmeg
2 Tbsp. melted butter
1 egg, beaten

In the slow cooker, place apples, sugar, dates, and pecans; stir. In a separate bowl, mix together flour, baking powder, salt, and nutmeg. Stir into apple mixture. Drizzle melted butter over batter and stir. Stir in egg. Set cooker on low and cook for 3 to 4 hours. Serve warm.

NOTE: If crispier nuts are desired, acid toasted pecans at the end of cooking period.

SIMPLE FUDGE SAUCE

MAKES 1 QUART

This easy fudge sauce can be used as a dessert fondue for dipping bananas, angel food cake, pound cake, etc. It also can be used as a delicious sauce over ice cream or cake.

12 oz. semi-sweet chocolate chips
¼ cup butter
2 cans (14 oz. each) sweetened condensed milk

⅓ cup liqueur—amaretto, orange-flavored, Frangelico, coffee or mint, optional

Place chocolate chips, butter, and condensed milk in the slow cooker. Turn cooker on low and cook for 1 to 2 hours; stir occasionally until chocolate melts. Stir in liqueur, if desired. Serve directly from slow cooker or serve warm over desserts. Store covered in the refrigerator for up to 2 weeks.

APRICOTS IN ALMOND LIQUEUR

SERVES 6

This is a quick and simple dessert that is delightful after a heavy meat.

1 can (19 oz.) whole apricots	½ cup amaretto liqueur
1 Tbsp. cornstarch	Toasted slivered almonds for garnish

Drain apricots and place juice in the slow cooker with cornstarch. Stir to dissolve. Turn cooker on low and allow mixture to thicken, half an hour to 1 hour. Add amaretto and cook half an hour longer. Pour sauce over apricots; cover and refrigerate for several hours. Garnish with a sprinkling of toasted almonds.

BUTTER SAUCE
MAKES 1 QUART

This is delicious over Cranberry Pudding, recipe on right.

1 cup sugar
½ cup butter
½ cup cream
1 tsp. vanilla or grated orange peel

In a heavy-bottomed saucepan or double boiler, slowly heat sugar, butter, and cream until sugar is dissolved. Using an electric mixer, whip at high speed until thickened. Stir in vanilla or grated orange peel.

CRANBERRY PUDDING
SERVES 8 TO 10

This is similar to steamed plum pudding, but more colorful and fresher tasting. If you freeze fresh cranberries when they are plentiful, you can have this dessert year-round. Top with Butter Sauce, see recipe on left.

2 cups fresh or defrosted frozen cranberries
1½ cups flour
½ cup molasses, preferably light
½ cup boiling water
2 tsp. baking soda
¼ tsp. salt
1 tsp. grated orange rind

Coarsely chop cranberries and mix with flour (this helps prevent the berries from sinking to the bottom of the pudding during steaming). Mix molasses, water, soda, salt, and orange rind together; stir into cranberries.

Grease a pudding mold or large coffee tin, pour in pudding mixture, cover with waxed paper and tie tightly with a string. Place in the slow cooker and pour water in to fill halfway up mold. Set cooker on high and cook for 5 to 6 hours. Check doneness by inserting knife in center. It should come out clean. Serve warm or at room temperature.

THIS & THAT
CEREALS, RELISHES, SAUCES, HOT BEVERAGES

KAMUT CEREAL

SERVES 4 TO 6

Kamut (say KAH-MOOT) is a highly nutritious wheat that contains a unique type of gluten easier for the body to utilize. Its grains are up to three times larger than wheat. It has more protein and potassium than wheat and it has a nutty, buttery flavor.

3 cups water
½ tsp. salt
1 cup whole grain kamut

Pinch cinnamon or nutmeg, raisins or chopped dates, grated orange rind, optional
Chopped toasted nuts, optional

Place water, salt, and kamut in the slow cooker and add any optional ingredients as desired. If you add nuts, do so after cooking so they won't become soggy. Set cooker on low and cook for 8 to 9 hours.

PARMESAN POLENTA

SERVES 6 TO 8

Polenta is a delicious alternative to potatoes or rice. It is simple to fix and can be chilled in loaf form to serve sliced with a tomato sauce.

2 cups polenta
6 cups boiling water
1 tsp. salt, or to taste

¼ cup butter
1 cup grated Parmesan cheese,
  preferably Asiago

Place polenta in the slow cooker; pour boiling water on top and stir. Add remaining ingredients and stir. Set cooker on low and cook for 1 to 2 hours, stirring occasionally until mixture thickens and is smooth and soft.

If you wish to serve polenta with a sauce, butter a loaf pan; pour in hot polenta and refrigerate until firm. Cut solid polenta into slices, place on a platter, heat in the oven until warm and top with Basil Tomato Sauce, page 83.

CRANBERRY CHUTNEY

MAKES 8 CUPS

Slow cookers are great for highly spiced fruit dishes like compotes and chutneys. Cranberry chutneys are best served with poultry and pork entrées and, of course, curry dishes.

4 cups fresh cranberries
1 cup water
½ cup golden raisins
½ cup dark raisins
2 cups sugar
1 tsp. ginger

1 tsp. cinnamon
½ tsp. allspice
Pinch cloves
½ tsp. salt
1 can (20 oz.) crushed pineapple,
   drained

Place all ingredients in the slow cooker and stir. Set cooker on low and cook for 4 to 6 hours. Taste and adjust seasonings.

NECTARINE CHUTNEY

MAKES 2 QUARTS

A fruit chutney like this goes well with Indian curries, as well as meat and fowl dishes. It can also be added to other sauces to bring out an unusual spiciness.

2½ lb. nectarines, peeled, pitted and sliced
1½ cups brown sugar
1 cup cider vinegar
¼ cup diced preserved ginger
1 Tbsp. salt, or to taste

¼ cup chopped onion
1 tsp. dry mustard
¼ tsp. cinnamon
⅛ tsp. cloves
½ cup slivered almonds, toasted

Place nectarines in the slow cooker with brown sugar, vinegar, ginger, salt, onion, mustard, cinnamon, and cloves. Stir mixture well, set cooker on low and cook for 3 to 4 hours, or until thick. Taste and adjust seasoning. Let chutney cool. Add almonds and refrigerate until ready to use. If desired, place mixture in a sterilized jar and process to heat seal.

PEACH PINEAPPLE CHUTNEY

MAKES 10 CUPS

Chutney is certainly becoming more popular, especially with increased interest in Indian cooking. This chutney goes well with wild game, lamb, curries, turkey, chicken, pork, or even ham.

5 cups peeled fruits — peaches, pineapple and apples
1 lemon, thinly sliced and seeded
2 cloves garlic, chopped
2¼ cups brown sugar

¾ cup crystallized ginger, chopped
2 tsp. salt
½ tsp. cayenne, or more to taste
2 cups cider vinegar
1 cup raisins, mixed dark and light

Mix any proportion of fruits and chop coarsely. Cut lemon slices into quarters and add to the slow cooker with fruits. Add remaining ingredients. Set cooker on low and cook for 4 to 6 hours. Stir occasionally to prevent scorching. After cooling, keep refrigerated until ready to use. If you choose to can, process for 5 minutes in a water bath after ladling into sterile jars.

NOTE: Ginger already adds heat to your recipe so be careful with the amount of cayenne.

BASIL TOMATO SAUCE

MAKES 3 CUPS

This is a fast simple sauce, made special with the addition of fresh basil.

¼ cup olive oil

3 cloves garlic, minced

2¼ cups canned plum tomatoes

Salt and pepper, to taste

15 fresh basil leaves, or 2 tsp. dried basil

Heat oil in a saucepan and gently fry garlic on medium until just golden but not brown. Chop tomatoes into small pieces, add to saucepan and cook on low, uncovered, until oil floats free on top. Add salt, pepper, and basil. If using fresh basil, take sauce off heat and stir in chopped fresh basil leaves. Taste and adjust seasonings.

PEANUT SAUCE (SATÉ SAUCE)

MAKES 4 CUPS

(Say SAH-TAY) This sauce is popular to serve with Thai marinated chicken or beef skewers. It's also good over lightly sautéed chicken and fresh spinach.

¼ cup oil
2 cloves garlic, minced
1 medium onion, chopped
½ tsp. chili powder
3 lime leaves
½ tsp. curry powder
1 Tbsp. chopped lemon grass
1 cup coconut milk

½ cup milk
¼ tsp. cinnamon
3 bay leaves
2 tsp. tamarind paste or 1 Tbsp. lemon juice
2 Tbsp. fish sauce
3 Tbsp. dark brown sugar
3 Tbsp. lemon juice
1 cup chunky peanut butter

Turn the slow cooker on high. Heat oil and add garlic, onion, chili powder, lime leaves, curry powder, and lemon grass. Cook until onion is tender. Turn cooker on low and stir in remaining ingredients. Cook on low for 2 to 3 hours or until thick.

NOTE: Fish sauce is available in Asian markets.

SPICED APPLESAUCE

MAKES 6 CUPS

Applesauce is becoming more popular as a substitute for high sugar sauces and syrups. A favorite alternative is to use applesauce on pancakes in the place of syrup. You can play with the spices for more variety.

12 apples, peeled, cored and sliced
½ cup sugar, or more to taste
2 Tbsp. lemon juice
1 tsp. grated lemon rind

1 stick (4 to 6 inch) cinnamon*
½ tsp. nutmeg
¼ tsp. allspice
Pinch cloves

Place all ingredients in the slow cooker and set on low. Cook for approximately 4 to 6 hours or until apples are tender. The time will vary depending on the type of apples used. Remove cinnamon stick. Taste and adjust seasonings. Serve warm or cold.

*I generally like to use a cinnamon stick because it doesn't darken the sauce as much, but you can substitute ½ tsp. cinnamon, or more, if you wish.

RHUBARB-STRAWBERRY SAUCE

MAKES 2 CUPS

This sauce can be served over ice cream, crepes or chocolate desserts.

8 oz. rhubarb
Water to cover
8 oz. strawberries

½ cup sugar, or to taste
2 Tbsp. lemon juice
1 tsp. grated lemon peel

Slice rhubarb and place in the slow cooker with enough water to cover. Set cooker on low and cook for 1 hour or until rhubarb is tender. Strain liquid from rhubarb and purée cooked rhubarb until smooth. Add strawberries, sugar, lemon juice, and peel. Purée until well mixed and smooth. Taste and adjust sweetness or tartness to personal preference.

HEALTHY APPLE BUTTER

MAKES 4 CUPS

For health-minded people, this recipe is sugarless, salt-free, and fat-free.
What more could you ask for?

8 lb. apples, peeled, cored and diced
1½ cups apple juice

2 tsp. cinnamon
1 tsp. nutmeg, or more to taste

Place apples in a blender or food processor with apple juice and blend until smooth. Transfer to the slow cooker, set on low, and cook for 6 to 7 hours. Stir occasionally. Let mixture cool; reblend and stir in spices. If desired, add more spices to taste. Store in the refrigerator after cooling to room temperature.

SWEET & SOUR APRICOT SAUCE

MAKES 2 QUARTS

This sauce is excellent for poultry, pork, and lamb dishes or as an accompaniment to Chinese dishes. When apricots are plentiful, make a large batch and process for future use.

6 cups pitted, chopped apricots
1 cup golden raisins
2 cups brown sugar
1 tsp. cinnamon
½ tsp. cloves
½ tsp. allspice

2 tsp. salt
¼ – ½ tsp. cayenne, optional
2 large onions, chopped
4 cloves garlic, minced
24 oz. Japanese preserved ginger
1½ cups cider vinegar

Place apricots, raisins, brown sugar, cinnamon, cloves, allspice, salt, and cayenne in the slow cooker and set on low. In a food processor or blender, purée onions, garlic, ginger, and vinegar until smooth. Add onion mixture to the slow cooker and stir. Cook for 3 to 4 hours, stirring occasionally, until the mixture is thick like ketchup. Taste and adjust seasonings. Store in the refrigerator until ready to use or process in sterilized jars to heat and seal.

COFFEE MEDITERRANEAN

SERVES 24

This mocha mixture, with a tinge of anise and cinnamon, is served hot with a twist of lemon and orange.

2 qt. hot coffee
¼ cup chocolate syrup
⅓ – ½ cup sugar
2 sticks (6-inch each) cinnamon
2 tsp. whole cloves

½ tsp. anise flavoring
Peel of 1 orange, cut into strips for garnish
Peel of 1 lemon, cut into strips for garnish
Whipped cream for garnish

Combine coffee, chocolate syrup, sugar, cinnamon, cloves, and anise flavoring in the slow cooker. Set on low and cook for 45 minutes to 1 hour. Float orange and lemon peel strips which have been tied into knots on top of mixture. Strain liquid into a cup and top each cup with a large dollop of whipped cream and strips of orange peel.

RUSSIAN TEA

SERVES 24

I'm always looking for new beverages to serve at parties. This is an unusual warm punch that mixes citrus, almond, and spices together.

2 cups sugar
2 cups water
2 cups orange juice
¼ cup lemon juice
½ gal. water

1 tsp. almond extract
2 tsp. vanilla extract
6 whole cloves
2 sticks (3-inch each) cinnamon

In a saucepan, boil water and sugar together for 5 minutes or until sugar dissolves completely. Pour into the slow cooker. Add remaining ingredients. Set cooker on low and cook for at least 1 hour before serving. Serve directly from slow cooker.

HOT BRAZILIAN EGGNOG

SERVES 24

Usually eggnog is served cold but the Brazilian version is served hot
and flavored with coffee.

4 eggs, separated
3 cups milk
2 cups cream
3 Tbsp. instant coffee
½ cup light corn syrup

½ cup brandy or rum, or to taste
¼ cup water
Pinch cinnamon, optional
Nutmeg for garnish, optional

With an electric mixer, beat egg yolks lightly; beat in milk, cream,
instant coffee, and ¼ cup corn syrup. Place mixture in the slow
cooker; set on low and cook for half an hour. Stir in brandy or rum.
In a saucepan, heat remaining corn syrup and water to a boil and
simmer for 5 minutes. Beat egg whites until soft peaks form and
slowly pour corn syrup mixture in a thin stream into eggs. Continue
beating until soft peaks form again. Fold mixture into hot milk
mixture. Ladle into punch cups or mugs and sprinkle with nutmeg,
if desired.

MULLED CIDER

SERVES 16

This is a sweet, spicy mixture that is loved by all, especially children.

¾ cup packed brown sugar
1 tsp. ground cloves
1 tsp. ground allspice
1 tsp. ground cinnamon

¼ tsp. salt
1 gal. apple cider
Cinnamon sticks, for garnish

Mix together the brown sugar, cloves, allspice, cinnamon, and salt. Place mixture in the slow cooker with apple cider on low until the sugar dissolves, approximately 20 to 25 minutes. Taste and if the mixture is too spicy, add more apple cider. Ladle into mugs and serve each cup of cider with a cinnamon stick.

INDEX